AN A TO Z OF
MONSTERS
AND MAGICAL BEINGS

Illustrations by Rob Hodgson
Text by Aidan Onn

Laurence King Publishing

ALIEN

The universe is gigantic and must be full of all kinds of weird and wonderful aliens living on faraway planets. They might even occasionally visit us on Earth. Perhaps some of the monsters in this book came from outer space and decided to stay. Which ones do you think might be aliens?

BANSHEE

Banshees wander the remote woodlands of Scotland and Ireland, wailing their warnings of deathly doom, and occasionally stopping to comb their long golden hair. If you hear a particularly woeful shrieking, it might be a banshee who has misplaced her comb (they can be quite forgetful). Should you ever find it—leave it be! Otherwise the banshees will scream at you.

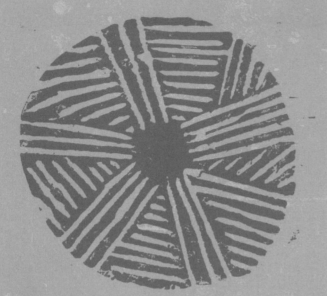

Cyclops

Stubborn and foul tempered, Cyclops are an ancient race of one-eyed giants. They are excellent blacksmiths, and the rumbling from inside a volcano is said to be the sound of them hard at work fashioning thunderbolts, which they will throw at you if they catch you staring.

DRAGON

These wise creatures can be found near wells, rivers, and caves, ferociously guarding their precious treasure. They are capable of human speech, but if you ever get talking to one, watch out for fiery spitballs. You must never slay a dragon and drink its blood: you'll become invincible, but your breath will smell terrible!

Eloko

These dwarf-like beasties live inside hollow trees, protecting the animals and plants of the African rainforests. They wear leaves and have grass for hair, piercing eyes, and long sharp claws. The Eloko ring little bells to entrance unwary hunters, so beware: if you go foraging in forests, always carry a lucky charm—or wear earplugs—to protect yourself.

Far darrig

These rascally fairies with long hair, short snouts, and skinny tails are known in Irish folklore as "Red Men" because of their fondness for bright red coats and caps. They always carry a shillelagh, which is a sharp wooden stick that's excellent for poking, prodding, and tripping up unwary travelers. Far Darrigs are very fond of practical jokes, so don't get in their way or there will be mischief.

GHOST

Ghosts are wispy shapes that float about
and disappear as soon as you notice them.
Often quite sad and solitary, they wander
around spooky old mansions and graveyards,
moaning and groaning and trying their best
to scare you away. Consider yourself very lucky
if you ever manage to befriend one.

Hobgoblin

Hobgoblins are small and hairy with sharp-pointed noses. They often hide in fireplaces, creeping out at night to do helpful odd jobs, and occasionally to misbehave (and eat all the cookies) if they are bored. You can always get rid of a troublesome hobgoblin by giving it a new set of clothes; pointy hats are a particular favorite. Why this works, nobody knows. Perhaps you could ask one!

IMP

These little pointy-tailed creatures are good friends with witches and enjoy riding on the back of broomsticks. Often wild and uncontrollable, they like to play pranks, such as switching babies or throwing clothes off the washing line. Although this "impishness" can be very annoying, they are really just looking for friendship and attention.

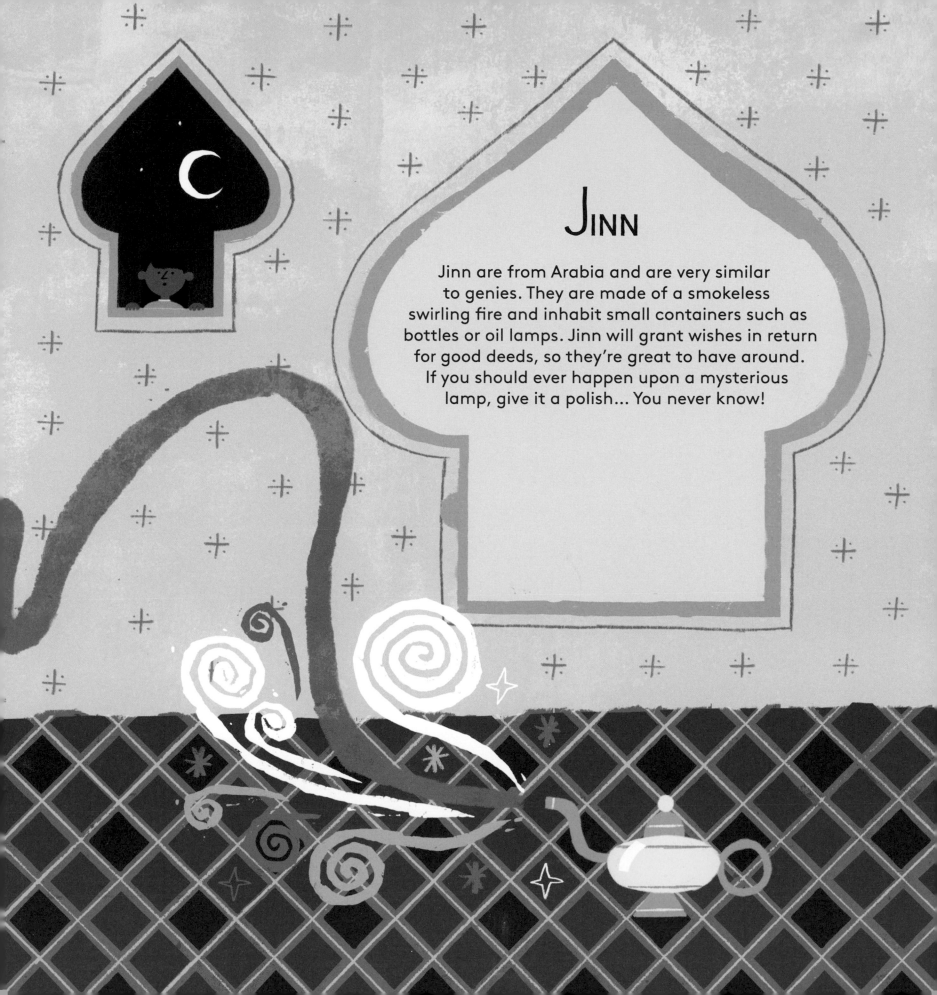

Jinn

Jinn are from Arabia and are very similar to genies. They are made of a smokeless swirling fire and inhabit small containers such as bottles or oil lamps. Jinn will grant wishes in return for good deeds, so they're great to have around. If you should ever happen upon a mysterious lamp, give it a polish... You never know!

Kraken

Salty sailors who have sailed the seven seas tell the tale of a gigantic sea monster—similar to an octopus—that swims off the coasts of Norway and Greenland. It attacks ships by wrapping its long tentacles around them and dragging them to the bottom of the ocean. The Kraken is so large that it is sometimes mistaken for a small island, but it's definitely not a good place to spend your holidays.

LEVIATHAN

This great fish is a sort of sea-dragon that lives deep beneath the waves and eats an entire whale for breakfast every day. The Leviathan has mighty fins, enormous horns, and very bright eyes. It is one of the biggest and meanest creatures to swim the seas: in a match between the Kraken and the Leviathan, the Leviathan would win hands (or rather fins) down.

Minotaur

In Greek mythology the Minotaur was a ferocious creature with the head of a bull and the body of a man, who lived in the center of a huge labyrinth built by King Minos of Crete. If you ever get lost in a mysterious maze, watch out! You might just meet this hungry beast. He will certainly gobble you up, unless you share your packed lunch with him.

Nessie

Loch Ness is one of the deepest lakes in Scotland and a mysterious serpentine monster lives at the bottom of it. Very occasionally she swims to the surface, but before anyone can get a good look or a decent photograph, she quickly disappears again. Locals have nicknamed her "Nessie," which she really likes.

Ogre

Ogres (and ogresses) are very large, ugly, smelly giants with unusually big heads and feet. Their round hairy bellies are fattened from eating their favorite delicacy, children (the badly behaved ones are especially tasty). But don't be too scared: ogres are almost always incredibly stupid, so clever children can easily outwit them and run away.

Pixie

Pixies are small, good-hearted fellows full of mischief. They have pointed ears and wear stylish green outfits with matching hats. Pixies mostly come out at night from their underground hideouts to dance, play harmless pranks, and sometimes wrestle with one another. Oh, and they do not like fairies!

QUESTING BEAST

This peculiar creature from the legend of King Arthur has the head and neck of a snake, the body of a leopard, the haunches of a lion, and the feet of a deer. Merlin, a wise wizard, thought its bark was so loud that it sounded like 30 hounds questing (an old word for hunting). King Arthur's knights never managed to catch the beast, so perhaps it's still hiding in the woods.

Roc

Arabian fairy tales tell of a bird of prey so large and so strong it can easily snatch up an elephant in its talons. Sailors have even said that the vengeful bird smashed their ships to pieces after they foolishly tried to steal its precious giant egg. Who could blame them? It would have made an excellent omelet and fed everyone twice over.

Sphinx

This demon, with the head of a woman, the body of a lioness, and the wings of an eagle, guards the entrance to the Greek city of Thebes. To enter, travelers have to solve her riddle: "What walks on four legs in the morning, two legs at noon, and three in the evening?" If they don't know, she swallows them in one giant gulp. Do you know the answer? (It's hidden somewhere in this book.)

TROLL

Scandinavian mountains are full of unfriendly trolls,
who hide out in isolated caves or under bridges.
If you find one, leave it be: they will eat anyone who
is foolish enough to disturb their snoring slumber.
Trolls have gnarled ugly faces and are very strong,
but they are generally slow and dim-witted, and
will turn to stone if they are ever caught in sunlight.

USHI-ONI

In ancient Japan fishermen were often chased away by an enormous crab-like sea monster with a horned buffalo head. An archer called Yamada Kurando Takakiyo eventually managed to kill the creature with a well-placed arrow. He gave the monster's horns to a temple on Shikoku Island where they are on display to this very day.

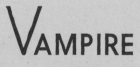

Vampire

These bat-like, sharp-toothed creatures rise
up out of their coffins at night to feast
on the blood of the living, returning to their
castles before dawn to sleep, always with
a wary left eye open. Unlike humans, they
cannot see their reflection in a mirror, and
they are scared of garlic and crucifixes.
A wooden stake through the heart will turn
them to ash.

Werewolf

The Old English word for a man was "were," so werewolves are humans who turn into wolves. Anyone unfortunate enough to be cursed by a witch, or bitten by another werewolf, will turn into a howling wolf whenever there is a full moon. It must be very annoying! Werewolves are tough, fearless creatures, but will run away in terror from silver objects—except the moon, of course!

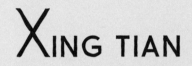

Xing tian

This brave Chinese giant got into a fight
with a very powerful supernatural being called
"The Yellow Emperor" and was beheaded during the
battle. Xing Tian's head rolled away into a deep valley
and was lost forever, but he refused to be beaten...
He continued the fight by growing new eyes and a mouth on
his gigantic belly. So be warned: giants are not easily defeated!

YETI

These very shy mountain creatures live
in the Himalayas and have been spotted
dashing through the remote forests and
foothills of the mountains, making a whistling,
swooshing sound as they pass. Very occasionally they
linger just long enough to be fleetingly photographed by
intrepid explorers. Perhaps they would stop for a selfie if you
offered them ice cream.

ZOMBIE

Often misunderstood, zombies actually have no interest in biting your arm or chewing your leg. They are slaves to the witch doctors who have brought them back to life in order to scare you, and help with witch-doctory chores. The only way to save a zombie and return it to the grave (should you be so inclined) is to feed it salt.

ALIEN

GHOST

HOBGOBLIN

JINN

BANSHEE

ELOKO

FAR DARRIG

DRAGON

LEVIATHAN

IMP

KRAKEN

MINOTAUR

CYCLOPS

Nessie

Vampire

Xing Tian

Questing beast

Werewolf

Pixie

Sphinx

Ushi-oni

Yeti

Roc

Ogre

Troll

Zombie

LAURENCE KING

First published in 2017 by
Laurence King Publishing Ltd
361–373 City Road
London EC1V 1LR
+44 20 7841 6900 (Tel)
+44 20 7841 6910 (Fax)
enquiries@laurenceking.com
www.laurenceking.com

Text by Aidan Onn
Illustrations © 2017 Rob Hodgson

A catalog record for this book is available from the
British Library.

ISBN: 978 1 78627 067 2

Design by Charlotte Coulais

Printed in China

The answer to the Sphinx's riddle is "humans." They crawl on all fours as babies in the "morning of life," walk upright on two legs during the middle part, or "noon of life," and need a walking stick in their old age—the "evening of life."